21st Century
Basic Skills
Library

BABY ZOO ANIMALS
CHIMPANZEES

by Katie Marsico

Cherry Lake Publishing • Ann Arbor, Michigan

3

Published in the United States of America
by Cherry Lake Publishing
Ann Arbor, Michigan
www.cherrylakepublishing.com

Content Adviser: Dr. Stephen S. Ditchkoff, Professor of Wildlife Sciences,
Auburn University, Auburn, Alabama

Photo Credits: Cover and page 1, ©Ronnie Howard/Shutterstock, Inc.;
page 4, ©Kitch Bain/Shutterstock, Inc.; page 6, ©Kodo34/Dreamstime.
com; page 8, ©Yfwong74/Dreamstime.com; page 10, ©Uryadnikov
Sergey/Shutterstock, Inc.; page 12, ©Sam Dcruz/Shutterstock, Inc.; page 14,
©Bluerain/Shutterstock, Inc.; page 16, ©Sharon Morris/Dreamstime.
com; page 18, ©Nick.biemans/Dreamstime.com; page 20, ©Noppadon
Chanruangdecha/Dreamstime.com

Library of Congress Cataloging-in-Publication Data
Marsico, Katie, 1980–
  Chimpanzees / by Katie Marsico.
    p. cm. — (21st century basic skills library) (Baby zoo animals)
  Includes bibliographical references and index.
  ISBN 978-1-61080-455-4 (lib. bdg.) — ISBN 978-1-61080-542-1 (e-book) —
ISBN 978-1-61080-629-9 (pbk.)
1. Chimpanzees—Infancy—Juvenile literature. 2. Zoo animals—Infancy—
Juvenile literature. I. Title.
  SF408.6.C53M38 2013
  599.885—dc23   2012001726

Cherry Lake Publishing would like to acknowledge
the work of The Partnership for 21st Century Skills.
Please visit www.21stcenturyskills.org for more information.

Printed in the United States of America
Corporate Graphics Inc.
July 2012
CLFA11

TABLE OF CONTENTS

A Lot Like Human Babies

Chimpanzees are **primates**.

They can use their hands and feet much like humans do. Their eyes face forward.

Chimps are found in Africa. They also live in zoos across the globe.

Chimps usually have only one baby at a time.

The babies share a close **bond** with their mothers. This is just like human babies!

A newborn chimp hangs on to its mother's stomach. This goes on for about a month after birth.

The baby later travels on its mother's back.

A Chimp's Day

Chimps at the zoo are most active during daylight hours.

They rest in tree branches at night.

Chimps eat fruits, berries, and small animals such as bugs.

Baby chimps also drink their mother's milk. They do this for 4 to 6 years after birth.

Baby chimps spend much of their day playing.

They tickle and chase one another.

Sometimes **zookeepers** let them play with balls and dolls!

Chimps **communicate** by making noises. They also make **gestures** with their faces and hands.

Mothers and babies often hug and kiss each other.

All Grown Up

Mother chimps and their babies often live together their whole lives.

This is true in the wild and at the zoo.

Female chimps are adults when they are about 12 years old. Then they are ready to have babies.

Then zookeepers welcome new baby chimps!

Find Out More

BOOK
Owen, Ruth. *Chimpanzees*. New York: Windmill Books, 2012.

WEB SITE
Chimp Haven
www.chimphaven.org/education/games-for-kids
This Web site features games, fast facts, and tips on how kids can help protect chimps in the wild.

Glossary

bond (BAHND) a close tie between two people or animals

chimpanzees (chim-pan-ZEEZ) apes with large ears and black fur

communicate (kuh-MYOO-ni-kate) share information, ideas, or feelings

gestures (JES-chuhrz) hand and body motions that express thoughts and feelings

primates (PRY-mates) mammals that have flexible hands and feet, good eyesight, and eyes that face forward

zookeepers (ZOO-kee-purz) workers who take care of animals at zoos

Home and School Connection

Use this list of words from the book to help your child become a better reader. Word games and writing activities can help beginning readers reinforce literacy skills.

a	branches	feet	kiss	old	tickle
about	bugs	female	later	on	time
across	by	for	let	one	to
active	can	forward	like	only	together
adults	chase	found	live	other	travels
Africa	chimp	fruits	lives	play	tree
after	chimpanzees	gestures	lot	playing	true
all	chimp's	hands	make	primates	up
also	chimps	hangs	making	ready	use
and	close	have	milk	rest	usually
animals	communicate	hours	month	share	welcome
another	day	hug	most	small	when
are	daylight	human	mother	sometimes	whole
as	do	humans	mother's	spend	wild
at	dolls	gestures	mothers	stomach	with
babies	drink	globe	much	such	years
baby	during	goes	new	the	zoo
back	each	grown	newborn	their	zookeepers
balls	eat	in	night	them	zoos
berries	eyes	is	noises	then	
birth	face	its	of	they	
bond	faces	just	often	this	

23

Fast Facts

Habitat: Rain forests and grasslands
Range: Africa
Average Height: 4 to 5.5 feet (1.2 to 1.7 meters)
Average Weight: 70 to 130 pounds (32 to 59 kilograms)
Life Span: About 45 years

Index

About the Author

Katie Marsico is the author of more than 100 children's and young-adult reference books. She could easily spend all day watching the chimps at her local zoo.